Disgustingly Delicious

Hilarious
treats to
freak out *your*
friends

Printed in the United States of America
by G&R Publishing Co.

Distributed By:

507 Industrial Street
Waverly, IA 50677

ISBN-13: 978-1-56383-382-3
ISBN-10: 1-56383-382-4
Item #2905

Icky Bugs
Don't worry, they won't bite... much.

Water Bugs Makes 5 bugs

5 Kalamata olives
30 long fresh rosemary leaves
10 short fresh rosemary leaves

These have just enough zippy flavor that you might stick out your tongue and hope for more. For each bug, roll 6 rosemary leaves between your fingers so they have a long, rounded shape. Pierce the olive with a tooth-pick in 3 places on each side for legs. Insert 1 rosemary leaf into each hole. Insert 2 short rosemary leaves in front for the antennae.

Roaches Makes 5 roaches

1⅓ T. cream cheese, softened, plus
    more for attaching legs and head
1 T. chopped walnuts

5 pitted dates
3 dried cherries

These roaches are sweet, crunchy and curiously chewy. To create your own, stir together cream cheese and walnuts. Cut 1 cherry in half and cut 6 thin legs from 1 half; use the other half to cut 5 roach heads. Cut 12 thin legs from each of the 2 remaining cherries. For each roach, pipe the cream cheese mixture into the hole at one end of the date. Attach the head and legs to each roach using more cream cheese.

Bug Bodies Makes 50-60 insects

1 (2 oz.) pkg. salted pistachios in their shells
Food coloring, optional

It's disgusting to pull the wings off headless insects and hear the "crunch" as you devour their bodies! Serve pistachios in their shells plain or colorize them by putting a few drops of food coloring into a resealable plastic bag and adding the pistachios. Close the bag and roll the nuts around in the bag to reach the desired "buggy" color. You can also add a drop of food coloring directly to their shells for an intense pop of color. Allow them to dry on paper towels. "Crunch-crunch."

Fido's Feast

Makes 9 cups of kibbles

It'll make your dog jealous!

You'll Need

4½ C. Kix cereal
4½ C. Corn Pops cereal
1½-2 C. Nestlé Nesquik powder
½ C. creamy peanut butter

¼ C. butter
1 C. milk chocolate chips
1 tsp. vanilla extract
1 large paper bag

Directions

Grrrr!

STEP # **1** In a large bowl, stir together the Kix and Corn Pops cereals.

STEP # **2** Put the Nesquik powder in the paper bag.

STEP # **3** In a small saucepan over low heat, combine the peanut butter, butter and chocolate chips until the chips are completely melted; then stir in the vanilla.

STEP # **4** Pour the melted mixture over the cereal mixture and stir it until all of the pieces of cereal are completely covered.

STEP # **5** Now dump the entire mixture into the paper bag with the Nesquik powder, and close the bag by folding over the top 2 or 3 times. Pick up the bag and walk to the sink. Are you at the sink? Good. (It's easier to clean the sink than the floor if there's a hole in the bag.) Now shake the bag vigorously to coat all of the pieces of dog food in chocolate powder.

Warning: Treat may cause a desire to chase cars, drink out of the toilet or bark uncontrollably!

Raunchy Rodents

Makes 8-10 beady-eyed rats

These ferocious pests gnaw on everything, but be warned—they don't like to be gnawed on!

You'll Need

2 lbs. ground beef

½ onion, chopped

1 egg, beaten

1 C. dry bread crumbs

1 (1.25 oz.) pkg. meatloaf seasoning mix

8-10 cubes Cheddar or mozzarella cheese, optional

8-10 pieces uncooked spaghetti

2 (15 oz.) cans tomato sauce

1 C. sugar

1 T. Worcestershire sauce

16-20 green peppercorns or frozen green peas

16-20 very thin carrot slices

Directions

Repulsive!

STEP # **1** Preheat the oven to 350°. Spray a 10 x 15" baking pan with nonstick cooking spray.

STEP # **2** To a large bowl, add the ground beef, onion, egg, bread crumbs and meatloaf seasoning. Use your hands to mix it all together.

STEP # **3** Measure ⅓ cup of the meat mixture for each rat. Push 1 cube of cheese inside, if you'd like. Shape the meat mixture around the cheese to form the rat's body, keeping one end rounded and the other end pointed (for the nose). Do this for the rest of the meat mixture. Place the rats in the baking pan, leaving about 4" between them.

STEP # **4** Break uncooked spaghetti into 4 equal pieces. Push 4 pieces of spaghetti into the rounded end near the bottom of each rat for the tail.

STEP # **5** In a medium bowl, stir together the tomato sauce, sugar and Worcestershire sauce. Pour this mixture over the rats and their tails; cover the pan with aluminum foil.

STEP # **6** Bake for 45 minutes; then remove the aluminum foil. Spoon some of the sauce from the pan over the rats and continue to bake uncovered for 20-30 minutes more. Remove the pan from the oven and move the rats to a serving tray, being careful not to break their tails (they hate that). Let them cool for a few minutes.

STEP # **7** Carefully press 2 peppercorns or peas into the pointy end of each rat to make the beady eyes. Press 2 carrot slices on top to make ears (you might need to cut slits into the top of the rat with a knife to help insert the carrots). Spoon a little sauce around the rats before serving.

Start by slurping up the tail and make your way to its beady little eyes . . . or maybe you want to start with the eyes so it can't watch as you devour it.

Eerie Floating Hand

Makes 16 cups of lemonade and 1 stone-cold hand

Be prepared for a round of high fives!

You'll Need

- 1 (32 oz.) bottle dark blue sports drink or other bottled beverage
- 2 (.23 oz.) pkgs. lemonade flavored unsweetened Kool-Aid drink mix
- Sugar and water as shown on Kool-Aid package directions
- 1-2 NEW, unused powder-free synthetic or latex gloves*
- 1 chip clip or several clothespins
- 1 2-qt. punch bowl or pitcher

Directions

Eeewww!

STEP # 1 The day before you want to serve the punch, thoroughly clean and rinse the inside and outside of the rubber glove. Dry the outside.

Get someone to help you with the next 2 steps, unless you have 4 hands. (Now that's creepy!)

STEP # 2 Carefully pour the sports drink into the clean rubber glove, filling it just past the wrist area. (There will be extra sports drink, so either drink up or make 2 hands, using the extra hand another time or just keep it in the freezer for some surprised reactions.)

STEP # 3 Fold over the opening of the glove 2 or 3 times and use a chip clip or several clothespins to pinch the fold and keep it in place. Put the filled glove on a plate or in a shallow bowl and set it in the freezer overnight.

STEP # 4 Mix up the lemonade following the package directions. Pour it into a punch bowl or pitcher and refrigerate for several hours or overnight.

STEP # 5 At serving time, take the frozen hand out of the freezer and carefully cut off the glove with scissors. Float the hand in the lemonade. Beware that as the hand begins to melt, the lemonade will turn an eerie, green color. What fun!

* If you use latex, be sure none of your guests have a latex allergy.

If the punch reaches up to give you a high five,
run for your life!

Creepy Crawlers

Makes 4 squirming sandwiches

If you've ever wondered how to eat grilled worms... (and, really, who hasn't wondered that!?)

You'll Need

6 bun-length hot dogs → the worms
4 hot dog or hamburger buns
Honey → the slime

Directions

Grimy!

STEP # **1** Preheat an indoor or outdoor grill to medium heat.

STEP # **2** Cut each hot dog in half the long way. Then cut each half in half again the long way so you have 24 long night crawlers.

STEP # **3** Place the worms on the grill rack and grill uncovered, turning occasionally to brown all sides. They will begin to curl as they cook. The longer they cook, the grungier they look.

STEP # **4** Remove from the grill and brush with a small amount of honey.

" Nobody likes me, everybody hates me,
I think I'll go eat worms..."

What tastes good on a creepy crawler sandwich?
Revolting Worm Goo, of course!

Revolting Worm Goo

Makes 1 cup
disgustingly delicious goo

You'll Need

½ C. ketchup
¼ C. prepared yellow mustard

¼ C. pickle relish

Directions

In a small bowl, stir together the ketchup, mustard and relish. Serve with Creepy Crawlers.

Dip 'em in it, cover 'em up or dab a little here and there ...
worms like to slither in goo!

The Litter Box

Makes 24 disgusting litter box servings

Follow this recipe closely and you'll have your friends eating out of... a litter box!

You'll Need

1 (18.2 oz.) pkg. spice cake mix

1 (18.2 oz.) pkg. white cake mix

Oil, eggs and water for both cakes as shown on packages

1 (3.4 oz.) pkg. vanilla instant pudding mix

Milk for pudding as shown on package

1 (25-32 oz.) pkg. cream-filled vanilla sandwich cookies

Green food coloring

Black food coloring, optional

Black writing gel, optional

14-20 mini Tootsie Rolls ← cat "poops"

1 NEW, unused kitty litter box

1 NEW, unused pooper scooper

Directions

P.U.!!

STEP # **1** Mix and bake both cakes following the package directions for any size cake. Remove the cakes from the oven; cool completely, then crumble both of them into a large bowl.

STEP # **2** Prepare the pudding mix following the package directions; refrigerate.

STEP # **3** Thoroughly wash and dry the litter box and pooper scooper.

STEP # **4** Finely crush the cookies. Stir half of them into the crumbled cake. Set aside ¼ cup of the remaining crumbs and put them into a small bowl. Add a few drops of green food coloring to the crumbs in the small bowl and stir until tinted green. Add a small amount of black food coloring and/or writing gel to mute the color a little.

STEP # **5** Stir the prepared pudding into the crumbled cake mixture until it's moist but not soggy (there's nothing worse than a soggy litter box – especially when you plan to eat out of it). Pour the cake mixture into the litter box.

STEP # **6** Remove the wrappers from the Tootsie Rolls and place a few at a time in a microwave-safe bowl. Heat them for a couple of seconds at a time until they're nice and soft but not melted. Roll and pinch the Tootsie Rolls until they look more like . . . well, cat "poops." Continue with the remaining Tootsie Rolls until they are all shaped the way you want them. Set aside 2 of them. Bury half the remaining poops in the cake mixture. Sprinkle with the remaining plain crushed cookies. Put the other half of the poops over the top.

STEP # **7** Sprinkle the green cookie crumbs randomly over the top of everything in the litter box. Lay the 2 set-aside poops over the sides of the litter box *(oops—naughty kitty)*. Place the litter box on a newspaper and use the pooper scooper to serve.

Now, just keep the cats away from THIS litter box, and everything will be just fine.

Brittle Bones

Makes 20 crunchy bones

No bones about it—they're creepy, and spine-tingling, and they crunch when you bite 'em.

You'll Need

5 large pretzel rods
10 thin pretzel sticks
20 regular marshmallows

20 mini marshmallows
12-14 oz. white almond bark

Directions

Bone Chilling!!

STEP # 1 Line a cookie sheet with waxed paper.

STEP # 2 Break the large pretzel rods in half.

STEP # 3 Smash all the marshmallows a little so they look more like the ends of bones and less like marshmallows.

STEP # 4 Push one end of a pretzel rod half through the long side of a regular marshmallow and do the same with the other end. Push one end of a whole pretzel stick through the long side of a mini marshmallow and do the same with the other end. Do this with all the pretzels and marshmallows. Be sure the ends of the pretzels aren't poking through the opposite side of the marshmallows.

STEP # 5 In a small microwave-safe bowl, melt the almond bark in the microwave until it's soft, but still has a few small lumps (the lumps will make the bones even creepier).

STEP # 6 Carefully place 1 bone at a time in the melted almond bark and use a spoon to ladle it over the bone until it is completely covered. Using a fork, lift the bone and hold it above the measuring cup for a few seconds to let the excess almond bark drip off. Set the bone on the prepared cookie sheet. Do this for all the bones. Set aside the remaining almond bark.

STEP # 7 Set the cookie sheet in the refrigerator for 30 minutes. If the almond bark looks too thin in some places, reheat the remaining almond bark and use a spoon to ladle a little of it over those areas (you don't want bare bones). Refrigerate again until the bones are dry. Store in a covered container.

Who knew munching on bones could taste so good?!
Rex knew all along! "Bone" appétit!

Cow Pie Delights

Makes about 8 large steaming cow pies

Hot out of the oven, these cow pies will steam just like the real thing.

You'll Need

1 (18.2 oz.) pkg. devil's food cake mix

2 eggs

½ C. vegetable oil

4 (2″) squares dark chocolate candy bar, broken in half

½ C. toasted coconut*

Directions

Squishy!

STEP # **1** Preheat the oven to 350°. Spray a baking sheet with nonstick cooking spray.

STEP # **2** In a medium bowl, stir together the cake mix, eggs and vegetable oil until well blended.

STEP # **3** Using at least 3 tablespoons of dough for each cow pie, place the dough on the prepared baking sheet in 3-3½" irregularly shaped mounds, making sure to place lumps of dough on top to give the cow pies that "just-plopped" look. Tuck a chocolate piece into each and add a little toasted coconut.

STEP # **4** Bake for 9 to 12 minutes or until the middle is done. Allow them to cool on the baking sheet for 5 minutes before moving to a cooling rack.

* To toast coconut, place in a dry pan over medium heat or on a baking sheet in a 350° oven for about 10 minutes, stirring occasionally to brown evenly.

Serve steaming hot or let them cool. You'd hate to admit you burned your tongue on a steaming cow pie!

Slippery Squid Dogs

Makes 12 long-legged squids

They're wiggly, jiggly and really cool to eat.

You'll Need

4 hot dogs → squid bodies
1 (8 oz.) pkg. uncooked spaghetti
   (you'll need 128 pieces) → squid arms
Ketchup or spaghetti sauce for
   dipping squid dogs, optional

Directions

Slurp!!

STEP # **1** In a large saucepan over high heat, bring 6-8 cups of water to a boil.

STEP # **2** Cut each hot dog in 4 even chunks to create bodies.

STEP # **3** Push 8 pieces of uncooked spaghetti arms through one cut side of each body and out the other side so the body is in the center of the arms. (You'll now have 16 squid dogs, with 8 arms sticking out each side.)

STEP # **4** When the water is boiling, turn the heat to medium and carefully place the squid dogs in the saucepan, pushing down gently to make sure they are completely covered with water. Cook for 11 to 13 minutes or until the arms are tender and wiggly.

STEP # **5** To serve, pile them up in a big bowl and tell your guests to dig in! Swirl them around in ketchup or spaghetti sauce before eating. Yum! Yum!

Slimy yet curiously satisfying!!

Putrid Piranha

Makes 1 outrageously dangerous fish

Do NOT—I repeat—do NOT put your fingers in its mouth! It's a meat eater, you know.

You'll Need

1 (1.7 lb.) pork center cut loin fillet
   (mesquite barbeque or other flavor)
10-12 strips bacon
15-20 slivered almonds → the Fangs
2 black olive slices → the Eyes

Directions

Vicious!

STEP # **1** Cut 3 strips of bacon in half crosswise. Lay half of these pieces over one short end of the fillet, overlapping the uncut sides of the bacon to cover the end of the fillet.

STEP # **2** Starting from the covered end of the fillet, wrap the long bacon strips around the fillet, overlapping the strips until the entire length of the fillet is covered. Lay the remaining short bacon pieces over the uncovered end of the fillet, tucking the ends under the bacon already wrapped around the fillet.

STEP # **3** Wrap the piranha in plastic wrap and curve it slightly if you'd like to give it a shapely figure. Freeze for about 4 hours.

STEP # **4** Preheat the oven to 350°. Spray a baking pan with nonstick cooking spray.

STEP # **5** Remove the plastic wrap from the piranha and place the piranha in the pan. Bake for about 1 hour and 20 minutes or until done.

STEP # **6** Remove from the oven and use a sharp knife to remove a chunk of meat from one short end to create a mouth shape. Pop that piece in your mouth before somebody else grabs it! Yummmm!

Time to make it mean-looking . . .

STEP # **7** Push the almonds side by side into the mouth area to create nasty-looking fangs. Create eyes using the olive slices.

STEP # **8** At serving time, start cutting off slices of the piranha, saving the mouth for last so your guests don't forget what they're eating . . .

4 added grossness!

Garnish with barbeque sauce and let your imagination take over. Add a few water bugs, too (see recipe pg. 3).

Icky Activities

Don't be afraid to get your hands dirty ...

Shrunken Heads

Remove most of the peel from 4 large apples. Cut the apples in half and take out the seeds and core. Using a small knife, carve a face on the round side of each half (cuts on the surface will be magnified after shrinking so do this carefully). Make the facial features large since their size will be reduced quite a bit. Now, stir together 1 cup of lemon juice and 1 tablespoon of coarse salt and immerse the apple halves in the mixture. Let them soak for 1 minute, and then place them on paper towels to drain. Lay the apples face-side up on a baking pan lined with parchment paper and bake at 250° for about 90 minutes. You can either toss these into drinks or coat them with polyurethane or shellac if you want to preserve them.

Drink a Cup of Blood

Pour ⅓ cup of water into a plastic cup. Add 1 teaspoon chocolate syrup, 3 teaspoons light corn syrup and 5-8 drops red food coloring. Mix well and drink up. This is sure to gross out your friends.

Barfy Book Covers

Blow up disgusting medical photos (intestines are particularly sickening) with a color copier to 200% and cover your textbooks with the icky innards. Hey, it's educational! But check the rules in your school first.

Paint w/ Bird Poop

Pour about ¼ cup white tempera paint into a squeeze bottle. Add small bits of crushed berries, seeds and nuts. Put the lid on the bottle, place your finger over the hole in the tip of the bottle and shake to mix. Spread a work area with newspaper and place a large piece of heavy black paper on the newspaper. Stand above the paper and squeeze the bottle to make splats of bird poop. Wait until the bird poop dries before hanging your creation in the window. Don't even think about taking a bite! Eating bird poop is ALWAYS a bad idea!

Touchy Feely Game

Cut a hole in the side of a box or brown paper bag just large enough for someone's hand to fit through. Cover the hole with a flap made of fabric or paper so your friends can't see inside but can still put their hand through. Put a variety of nasty items into the box or bag and let your friends feel around with their fingers. Because they're only using their sense of touch, it's a freaky game. Tell them what they might be feeling (see items in parentheses below) or just let their imaginations go wild. Dim the lights and play scary music to intensify the fear. Some ideas to put inside the box or bag:

Dried apricots (dried, shriveled tongues); cooked, cooled spaghetti (worms or veins); peeled grapes or cocktail onions (eyeballs); tines from a plastic fork or candy corn (vampire teeth); soft flour tortilla rubbed with a little oil or wrinkled fruit roll-ups (skin); field corn or corn nuts (teeth); corn silk or cooked and cooled spaghetti squash (hair); dried apple slices (ears); pumpkin membranes (guts); peeled tomatoes (hearts); cooked rice (maggots); banana chips (scabs); fresh green beans or carrots, peeled and dried (fingers); rubber glove filled with flour (dead hand); canned pear half or a chunk of ham carved into a tongue shape (tongue, obviously); cooked tapioca (frog eggs); prepared macaroni and cheese or oatmeal (brains); sunflower seeds (fingernails); meatballs in the shape of poop (you guessed it); hot dogs hooked together by their casings and covered in ketchup or cooked manicotti shells stuffed with sour cream (intestines).

Scary, Icky Story

Using some ideas from the Touchy Feely Game, tell a scary story. At different times throughout the story, pass around an item(s) that corresponds to that part of the story.

No Guts, No Glory

Fill a large container with lots of cooled cooked spaghetti or congealed gelatin. Bury plastic prizes or candies protected in resealable plastic bags in the container of spaghetti or gelatin. Blindfold your friends and have them dig through the guts for their prizes.

Brain Food

Makes 1 edible cranium

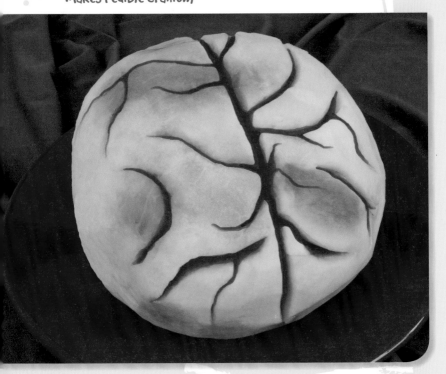

Any melon head would like this!

You'll Need

1 small seedless watermelon ⟶ the Brain

A picture of a brain to use as a guide

Directions

STEP # **1** Determine which side you want to carve. If necessary, cut a small slice off the opposite side so the melon sets flat.

STEP # **2** Using a sharp knife, **carefully peel** most of the green outer layer away from the watermelon, exposing the white layer below. Cut away most of the white layer in a few areas to expose a light pinkish color.

STEP # **3** Using the brain picture as a guide, **score** lines on the melon with a toothpick.

STEP # **4** With a sharp paring knife, **carefully carve** the scored lines, cutting away the white layer and exposing the melon's flesh.

STEP # **5** Serve **immediately**.

4 added grossness!

At serving time after your guests have had a chance to appreciate your master carving skills, begin "dissecting" the brain by cutting through the carved layer and exposing the "fleshy goodness" inside. Dig in!

It's a no-brainer!

Ogre Dentures

Makes 6 rotten grins

Pucker up for this lip-smackin' snack that'll make your friends happy they visit the dentist.

You'll Need

6 pink Laffy Taffy candies → **the Gums**
½ C. butterscotch chips
½ C. peanut butter chips
1 (1 oz.) square white baking chocolate
1½ tsp. shortening, divided
18-24 candy corn candies → **the Teeth**

Directions

ogre-licious!!

STEP #1 Soften 1 Laffy Taffy at a time in the microwave for about 5 seconds. Round off the edges slightly.

STEP #2 Carefully push the small end of 3 or 4 pieces of candy corn into one of the long sides of the Laffy Taffy, lining the candy corn up like teeth and breaking one off to resemble a broken tooth if you'd like. Repeat with the remaining candy corn and Laffy Taffy.

STEP #3 Place butterscotch chips, peanut butter chips and baking chocolate in 3 separate small microwave-safe bowls. Add ½ teaspoon shortening to each bowl. Heat them in the microwave until the chips are melted, stirring occasionally. The mixtures should be slightly thin. If they're not, add a little extra shortening and stir to melt. Let them cool slightly.

STEP #4 Use a spoon to drizzle the warm coating over the candy corn teeth, using a toothpick or butter knife to show separation between each tooth. Mix and match the colors to create different levels of tooth decay.

STEP #5 Repeat the process with remaining candy corn and Laffy Taffy.

" ... your hair turns gray, your teeth decay, and that is the end of a perfect day!"

Try 'em on for size and see how you'd look if YOU had rotting ogre Dentures!

Dough Toes

Makes about 64 unmanicured toes

They're short and stubby, crusty and disgusting—they're dough toes!

You'll Need

1 (11 oz.) roll refrigerated breadstick dough ———> the Toes

32 sliced almonds ———> the Ugly Toe Nails

1 egg white

Directions

STEP # **1** Preheat the oven to 350°. Line a baking sheet with parchment paper. Place the egg white in a small bowl and beat gently.

STEP # **2** Unroll each breadstick and cut each into pieces about 1-1½" long.

STEP # **3** Form each piece into the shape of a stubby toe, rounding the edges as desired. Place toes on the prepared baking sheet. Using kitchen shears, snip the dough gently in a few places where the knuckle will be.

STEP # **4** Break the almonds in half crosswise and place each half near one end of each toe, broken edge facing out for the toe nails. Press them into the dough so they stay in place while they bake.

4 added grossness!
Serve with Toe Jam Dip.

STEP # **5** Brush each toe with egg white and bake for 13 to 14 minutes or until done.

Dip your toes (eh, dough toes, that is) right into this dip or use a knife... either way, it's gonna be gross!

Toe Jam Dip

Makes about 1 cup of gooey, lumpy toe jam

You'll Need

⅓ C. peanut butter
⅓ C. honey

¼-⅓ C. tiny pieces cut from marshmallows

Directions

In a small bowl, stir together the peanut butter, honey and marshmallow pieces. Serve with Dough Toes.

Nothing's more disgusting than that stuff you find between your toes. Wanna see how it tastes?

Dirt Balls

Makes 24 dirty, gooey globs

It looks like you dropped them on the ground, rolled them in the dirt and decided to serve them anyway. Why not!?

You'll Need

24 regular marshmallows
¾ C. light corn syrup
1½-2 C. crushed candies,
    cookies and cereals* → the Dirt & Random Garbage
12 pink Starburst candies, unwrapped → the Bubblegum

Directions

filthy!

STEP # 1   Line a cookie sheet with waxed paper.

STEP # 2   Roll each marshmallow around in your hands, molding it so it looks like a lopsided glob. Repeat with the remaining marshmallows.

STEP # 3   Pour the corn syrup in a small bowl. Put crushed candies, cookies and cereals into individual small bowls. Roll Starbursts around in your hands (or heat in the microwave for a few seconds) until they're soft and pliable. Pull pieces off, mold them to look like chewed-up pieces of gum and set them on a small piece of waxed paper.

STEP # 4   Insert a toothpick into one of the marshmallows and dip it into the corn syrup. Immediately stick on one of the Starburst pieces and then dip in (or sprinkle with) candies, cookies and cereals, creating a randomly dirty-looking gooey glob. Repeat with the remaining marshmallows. Serve immediately or allow the syrup to set. Serve with toothpicks.

* We used candy rocks, toffee pistachios, Oreos and shredded wheat biscuits.

The "5-second rule" applies here!

Mice in Poo

Makes 16-18 scurrying mice

Mice... Mice in poo... Eeewww!

You'll Need

4 (1 oz.) squares semi-sweet
   baking chocolate

⅓ C. sour cream

1⅓ C. finely crushed chocolate
   wafers, divided

24 round decorating candies

24 sliced almonds

12 pieces red or black
   string licorice

Directions

Gross!!

STEP # **1** In a small microwave-safe bowl, heat the chocolate in the microwave until it's melted. Stir in the sour cream and 1 cup of the crushed chocolate wafers. Mix well. Cover and refrigerate until firm, about 1 hour.

STEP # **2** Using 1 tablespoonful of dough, roll the dough into balls. Form each into a slight point on one end for the nose. Roll the dough balls in crushed chocolate wafers to make them look extra brown and furry.

STEP # **3** For each mouse, press in 2 decorating candies to create eyes, 2 almonds to resemble ears and a tail made from licorice. Repeat for the remaining critters.

STEP # **4** Refrigerate for 2 hours before serving.

4 added grossness!

Add crushed graham crackers and chocolate decorating sprinkles to a tray or the inside of a box to represent sawdust and "mouse poo." To serve, place the mice on the tray or in the box and watch your friends get grossed out!

what do mice do-do?

Monster Q-Tips

Makes 10 really filthy cotton swabs

Somebody left their dirty Q-tips lying around! Put them to use as a tasty snack!

You'll Need

18 cream-filled vanilla
    sandwich cookies

1½ C. pecans

2 T. orange juice

3 T. light corn syrup

6 T. creamy peanut butter

3-4 squares white almond bark

2 T. apricot jam

1 T. creamy or crunchy
    peanut butter

10 (6-8") white cookie sticks

Directions

Putrid!

STEP # 1 Line a baking sheet with waxed paper.

STEP # 2 Finely crush the cookies and pecans and pour them into a large bowl. Stir in the orange juice, corn syrup and 6 tablespoons peanut butter; mix well.

STEP # 3 Shape the cookie mixture into 20 (1") balls and put 1 on each end of a cookie stick. Press the balls firmly forming them into long oval shapes to resemble the ends of Q-tips. Put them in the freezer for 30 minutes.

STEP # 4 In a small microwave-safe bowl, heat the almond bark in the microwave until it's melted. Cool slightly.

STEP # 5 Holding a chilled Q-tip by the stick, dip each end into the melted almond bark, coating the cookie completely and turning it to swirl the almond bark. Set each over a drinking glass or small bowl to allow the almond bark to dry. Do this for all of the Q-tips.

STEP # 6 Heat the jam in the microwave for a few seconds to soften it. In a small bowl, stir together the jam and the remaining 1 tablespoon of peanut butter. Dip the tips of both ends of the dried Q-tips into the "ear wax" to serve.

Quick Tip: For a quick way to make "clean" Q-tips, use white almond bark, Starburst candies and shorter lollipop sticks. Melt almond bark; cool slightly. Soften Starbursts and shape into ovals. Attach one to each end of a lollipop stick. Dip each Starburst into melted almond bark. Allow to set before serving.

After the first bite, your friends will be asking for more Q-tips ... and even extra ear wax!

Creepy Eyeballs

Makes 20 look-me-in-the-eye-when-I'm-talking-to-you cookies

It's eery when your food can watch you eat.

You'll Need

3 (1 oz.) squares white baking chocolate, divided

20 vanilla wafer cookies

Blue paste food coloring

20 M&M's mini baking bits or semi-sweet chocolate chips

Red liquid food coloring

1 small resealable plastic bag

Directions

Aagghh!!

STEP # **1** Line a baking sheet with waxed paper.

STEP # **2** In a small microwave-safe bowl, heat 2 squares of white chocolate in the microwave until they're melted.

STEP # **3** Holding a vanilla wafer rounded side up on a fork, ladel white chocolate over the top. Hold it above the bowl to let the excess drip off. Set the cookie rounded side up on the baking sheet. Repeat with the remaining cookies. Refrigerate until the white chocolate is set.

STEP # **4** Melt the remaining 1 square of white chocolate. Tint it using the blue food coloring and put it into the resealable plastic bag. Using scissors, carefully cut a small piece from one corner of the bottom of the bag. Squeeze a small amount of blue chocolate on the center of each cookie for the iris and place a mini baking bit in the center for the pupil. Refrigerate until set.

STEP # **5** Use a toothpick dipped in red food coloring to draw lines creating bloodshot eyes. Chill until set.

If you wink, will they wink back?

Fish Bowl

Makes enough for 8 slurping friends

Instead of cleaning the fish bowl, just invite some friends over. Add straws and enjoy!

You'll Need

→ Rocks & Fish Eggs

½ C. small pearl tapioca

Green, yellow and blue food coloring

4 T. sugar

Club Soda*

Lemonade*

Gummy fish

Green Rips bite-size licorice pieces, optional ← Seaweed

Lemon and orange zest, optional ← Fish food

Fish bowl**

Small funnel, optional

Directions

STEP # **1** Bring 6 cups of water to a boil and add the tapioca. Boil over medium heat, stirring occasionally, for about 20 minutes.

STEP # **2** Divide the tapioca and the remaining water evenly between 2 small bowls. To 1 bowl, add a couple drops of both yellow and green food coloring. To the other bowl, add 4 drops of blue food coloring. Add 2 tablespoons of sugar to each bowl and stir to dissolve the sugar.

STEP # **3** Leave the bowls uncovered and undisturbed for about 20 minutes. Then drain and rinse the tapioca under cold water until the water runs clear.

STEP # **4** Spoon the tapioca into the fish bowl.

STEP # **5** Cut the Rips into strips (hey, that rhymes) without cutting all the way through, leaving one end intact to create seaweed. Add the fish and the seaweed to the fish bowl, attaching*** the fish to the side of the bowl and anchoring the seaweed in the tapioca.

STEP # **6** At serving time, use a funnel or the back of a spoon to direct the flow as you slowly add Club Soda and lemonade to the fish bowl. The ratio is up to you, but in order to see the details inside the fish bowl, you should use mostly Club Soda with just a little lemonade. The more lemonade, the murkier the fish bowl.

STEP # **7** Sprinkle with lemon and orange zest to look like fish food if you'd like.

* Or the drink of your choice.

** No fish bowl? Just use a punch bowl, large glass bowl or pitcher instead.

*** Try using a small piece of Chuckles candy (the same color as the fish) to attach the fish to the inside of the fish bowl.

No backwash allowed if you're sharing!!

Gnarly Fingers

Makes 30-40 twisted fingers

*Fragile fingernails and gnarled knuckles—
what could be better?*

You'll Need

2-3 T. red liquid food coloring
30-40 whole almonds ⟶ **the fingernails**
2 eggs
¼ tsp. vanilla extract
½ C. butter, softened   5 T. sugar
½ C. powdered sugar   ⅛ tsp. salt
                                         1⅔-2 C. flour, divided

Directions

Finger-Lickin' Good!!

STEP # 1 Place food coloring in a small bowl. Dip 1 side of each almond into the food coloring. Place the almonds on paper towels to dry.

STEP # 2 Separate the yolk from the white of 1 egg. Discard the white or save it for something else. In a small bowl, whisk together the yolk, the other whole egg and the vanilla. In a mixing bowl, beat the butter, powdered sugar, sugar and salt until creamy. Add the egg mixture and beat until smooth. Add about 1⅔ cups of flour and stir just until the flour is mixed in. Cover and refrigerate for about 30 minutes.

STEP # 3 Preheat the oven to 350°. Line a baking sheet with parchment paper.

STEP # 4 Remove a small amount of dough at a time from the refrigerator. On a floured surface, roll about 1 teaspoon of dough into a finger shape, mixing in more flour as needed to make it stiff. Push up the dough for the knuckles and mark lines in those places with the back of a butter knife. Move fingers to the baking sheet. Press a red almond near the end of each finger for the fingernail, pushing the dough gently around the edges of the fingernail to make unsightly hangnails, if you'd like. Repeat with remaining dough.

STEP # 5 Bake until lightly browned, about 12 minutes. Move to a cooling rack.

4 added grossness!
Serve with Slimy Snot.

Slimy Snot

Makes more than enough for anybody's pickin'

You'll Need

1 C. white frosting

Blue and yellow plus red and/or black food coloring

Directions

Stir the frosting and add food coloring until it's a nice snotty green color.

No "real" nose-picking allowed!

Wiggling Worms

Makes 80 to 100 ooey, gooey disgustingly delicious worms

If your friends can slurp up these slimy worms without getting grossed out, they deserve an award.

You'll Need

1 (6 oz.) pkg. raspberry or grape gelatin

3 (.25 oz.) pkgs. unflavored gelatin

¾ C. whipping cream

10-20 drops green liquid food coloring

80-100 flexible plastic straws

Tall, narrow container, at least 4-cup capacity*

Directions

GAG!!

STEP # 1 In a medium bowl, combine flavored and unflavored gelatin. Add 3 cups of boiling water, stirring to dissolve completely. Chill at least 30 minutes or until nearly cool.

STEP # 2 Stir in the whipping cream until it's well mixed. Add food coloring until it reaches the desired "shade of worm".

STEP # 3 Pull on both ends of the straws to fully extend them and place all of them upright in the container with the shorter end of the straw facing down. Pour the gelatin mixture over the straws. Cover the container and refrigerate for at least 8 hours.

STEP # 4 Line a work surface and 2 large pans with waxed paper.

STEP # 5 Remove the straws from the container and place 5 or 6 at a time under hot running water for just a couple of seconds. Place them on a towel so the straws dry. Do this with all of the straws.

STEP # 6 Place 2 or 3 straws side by side on the waxed paper-lined work surface. Using a rolling pin, press firmly and roll from one end of the straws to the other, forcing the worms from the straws. Carefully move the worms to the waxed paper-lined pans and throw away the straws. Do this for all the worms and straws. Cover and chill for at least 2 hours. Carefully pile them up in a shallow bow and serve immediately.

*Find an upright container that's large enough for all of the straws but not too large - there shouldn't be a lot of extra "wiggle room" (pun intended). For easy removal, try using a disposable waterproof container like a 1-quart milk carton that can be cut away.

4 added grossness!

To make the worms even slimier, in a small bowl, stir together 1 cup purchased strawberry glaze (from a 13.5 ounce container) and ½ cup Mountain Dew until well combined. Brush or spoon the mixture over the worms. Serve immediately.

Icky Experiments

Don't freak out - there's no homework.

Slime or Snot
(depending on your level of grossness)

Dissolve ⅛ cup of borax in 2 cups of warm water. In another container, stir together 2 teaspoons of glue gel (white glue can be used but with a slightly different outcome) and 3 teaspoons of water. Add a few drops of food coloring to the glue mixture if you'd like. Stir well. In a resealable plastic bag, combine the borax mixture and the glue mixture and seal the bag. Squish it around in the bag until it becomes slimy. (There will be an excess of water remaining in the bag.) Remove the slime from the bag. The mixture will be wet, stringy and messy at first, but the more you handle it, the drier it becomes. If the texture isn't quite right after kneading, mix 1 part borax with 10 parts water; dunk the slime into this solution, remove it and knead it some more. Store your slime in a resealable plastic bag in the fridge with the words "DO NOT EAT" written on the bag. (Try blowing dust across the surface – it should form particles that could be mistaken for "boogers.")

Disappearing Egg Shell

Place a whole raw egg into a glass jar and cover the egg with white vinegar. Put a lid on the jar and let the egg set in the vinegar for 24 hours. Then pour out the vinegar and add fresh vinegar to the jar. Put the lid on again and let it set undisturbed for 7 days. Pour out the vinegar and carefully rinse the egg under cold water. The shell should be gone. Do not eat the egg! (Not that you'd want to.)

Germ Gardens

Find dirty places like your toes or a pet's cage, for instance, and some "seemingly" clean places like the kitchen counter. Write the location of each of these places on clean resealable plastic bags, one for each location. Put on a pair of rubber gloves and wipe slices of white bread (the kind without preservatives works best) over those surfaces. Place each slice of bread in the corresponding bag. Sprinkle each slice of bread with one teaspoon of water and seal the bag. Place the bags in a sunny area and watch over a period of time as mold begins to grow on each. This mold is just for observation! Because of possible allergies, do not open the bags at any time, and be sure to throw them away once you've observed how the molds differ in size and grossness. Eating the "moldy bread" on pgs. 50-51 is OK; eating THIS moldy bread or any other IS NOT!

Rubber Egg

Place a hard-cooked egg into a glass jar and cover the egg with white vinegar. Follow the directions for Disappearing Egg Shell (see recipe pg. 44). After 7 days, remove the egg and rinse under cold water. The egg will bounce. Again, do not eat the egg!

Dust Bunnies

Makes 4 dirty servings

For a casual dessert, simply sweep the floor, plop the dust pan down on the table and serve. (Or maybe you should follow this recipe instead.)

You'll Need

1 (3.9 oz.) pkg. chocolate instant pudding mix

2 C. milk

⅓ C. Oreo cookie crumbs, about 3 cookies

⅓ C. powdered sugar

1 NEW, unused dust pan

Directions

STEP # 1 In a small bowl, combine the pudding mix and the milk, whisking for 2 minutes or until it's well combined and the pudding begins to thicken. Refrigerate until serving time.

STEP # 2 Finely crush the cookies and stir together with the powdered sugar, being careful not to mix too completely.

STEP # 3 Thoroughly wash, rinse and dry the dust pan. Randomly spoon the pudding into the clean dust pan.

STEP # 4 Sprinkle the cookie mixture over the pudding. Serve immediately.

4 added grossness!

Add a roach or two to the dust pan before serving (see recipe pg. 3).

Serve immediately so someone doesn't take your dessert out to the trash can.

Brain Teaser

Makes 1 numb noggin'

You've heard the saying " pick somebody's brain" . . . now it's your turn to do it.

You'll Need

1 head cauliflower ———→ the Brain
2 C. salsa ———→ the Blood
1 C. guacamole dip
Tortilla chips ———→ the Brain Matter

Directions

Sick!!

STEP # 1 Remove the leaves from the cauliflower and carefully cut out most of the stem, leaving the outside intact. This will create a hollow area in the middle. Use toothpicks to help hold the outside together if you need to.

STEP # 2 Using a toothpick or a tiny paint brush dipped in the salsa, "draw" veins by following some of the natural lines in the cauliflower.

STEP # 3 Pour salsa into a shallow bowl or pan until the bowl is nearly full.

STEP # 4 Set the cauliflower in the middle of the salsa with the hollow side facing up.

STEP # 5 Fill the hollowed-out area of the cauliflower with the guacamole dip.

STEP # 6 Serve with chips.

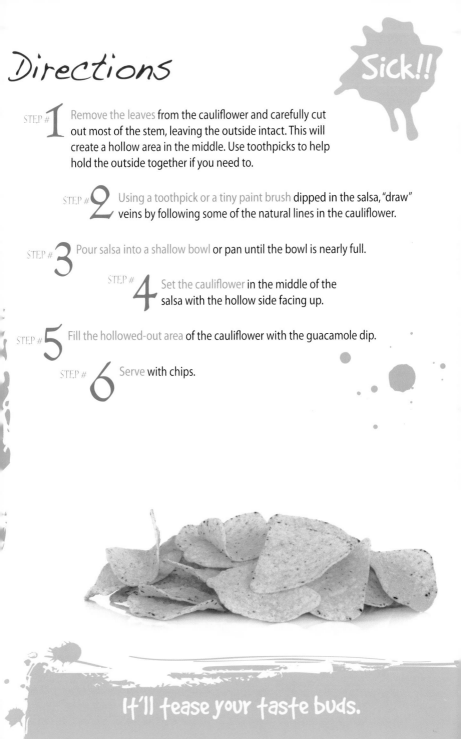

It'll tease your taste buds.

A Fungus Among Us

Makes 1 fantastically fungal sandwich

These sandwiches are certainly spoiled, but in a completely different way than your baby sister.

You'll Need

Butter
Sugar
Black, green and
   red food coloring

2 slices bread, any type
Peanut butter
Jelly
2 small resealable plastic bags

Directions

Vile!!

STEP # **1** In a small resealable plastic bag, combine 1 teaspoon of sugar with a small amount of black food coloring. Roll the bag and its contents around between your fingers until the sugar is a nice, gray color. You may need to add more sugar or more food coloring, depending on your preference of color.

STEP # **2** In another small resealable plastic bag, combine 1 teaspoon of sugar with 2 drops of green food coloring and 1 drop of red food coloring, rolling the bag and its contents between your fingers until it reaches a nice moldy-green color. Again, adjust the amounts to your preference.

STEP # **3** Using a tiny amount of butter as "glue", spread "spots" of butter on the bread where you'll want your "mold". Don't use too much butter or you'll end up with "wet mold" which is messy and not necessarily attractive. (But then, mold isn't really attractive anyway, is it?)

Now you can be creative...

STEP # **4** Using a small amount of the gray sugar and a small amount of the moldy-green sugar, sprinkle the mixtures over the butter-glue areas, gently pushing in the colors, mixing and layering until you get the look you want. Shake or brush off the excess sugar. You don't want any visible "sugar crumbs" left on the bread.

STEP # **5** Spread the non-moldy side of the bread with peanut butter and jelly, slap the 2 pieces together and serve the sandwich to your victim.

Why let those moldy slices of bread go to waste when you can feed them to your friends?

Tongue Twisters

Makes 2 tongues – 1 pink, 1 red

"These thousand tricky tongue twisters trip thrillingly off the tongue." Can you say it fast 3 times?

You'll Need

1 pink Laffy Taffy candy, unwrapped → the Pink Tongue

1 red Air Heads candy, unwrapped → the Red Tongue

2 wooden popsicle sticks

Directions

STEP # **1** Put the Laffy Taffy and Air Heads candies in the microwave for a few seconds at a time, until they're just slightly softened.

STEP # **2** Press each softened candy immediately onto a popsicle stick. The Laffy Taffy will adhere easily, but you'll need to press the bottom of the Air Head around the stick since it's less sticky. The higher you place the candy on the stick, the floppier the top of the tongue will be; the lower it's placed, the less floppy it will be.

STEP # **3** Stretch and shape each candy to form a tongue shape using the back of a spoon or your fingers. Then, using a toothpick, press a line down the center of the tongue.

STEP # **4** The Laffy Taffy will look like it has taste buds. To create taste buds on the Air Head, push down lightly on the Air Head using a meat mallot, a microplane or a box grater.

This is why your mother told you to never stick out your tongue!

Zombie Eyes

Makes 12 eggs that will watch your every move

Keep watching them — they NEVER blink!

You'll Need

6 eggs
¼ C. mayonnaise
¼ tsp. dry mustard
⅛ tsp. salt
⅛ tsp. paprika
⅛ tsp. garlic powder

Blue food coloring
12 black olive slices
12 pimentos or sweet red bell
    pepper pieces
Red liquid food coloring

Directions

STEP # 1 Place the eggs in a small saucepan and cover them with cold water. Bring the water to a full rolling boil over high heat. Cover the saucepan, remove it from the heat and let it set for 15 minutes. Drain the water and cover the eggs in the pan with cold water and several ice cubes. Let them stand about 10 minutes or until cool enough to handle.

STEP # 2 Peel the hard-cooked eggs and slice them in half lengthwise. Remove the yolks and transfer them to a medium bowl; set the whites aside.

STEP # 3 Using a fork, mash the yolks. Add the mayonnaise, dry mustard, salt, paprika and garlic powder; mix well.

STEP # 4 Add a few drops of blue food coloring and mix well to turn the yolks an eerie green. Divide the green yolk mixture evenly between the holes in the egg white halves.

STEP # 5 Position 1 black olive slice on each yolk-filled egg to resemble the iris. Add a pimento or piece of bell pepper to the center of the olive to resemble the pupil.

STEP # 6 Cover and chill in the refrigerator until serving time.

STEP # 7 Just before serving, use a toothpick dipped in red food coloring to draw veins on the egg white to resemble bloodshot eyes.

Don't make eye contact with these guys . . .
they're Zombies!

Cold-Blooded Reptile

Makes 1 Luscious Lizard

Cold-blooded, but filled to the brim with warm and gooey insides.

You'll Need

2 (8 oz.) rolls refrigerated
  crescent roll dough
Flour for dusting
½-1 C. pizza sauce
½ lb. Italian sausage cooked,
  crumbled and drained, or
  your choice of toppings

1 C. shredded
  mozzarella cheese
½ C. grated Parmesan cheese
1 egg yolk
2 black olive slices
2 red peppercorns
2 black peppercorns
1 roasted red pepper

the Eyes
the Nostrils
the Forked Tongue

Directions

STEP # **1** Preheat the oven to 375°. Line a large baking pan with aluminum foil and spray the foil with nonstick cooking spray.

STEP # **2** Unwrap 1 roll of crescent roll dough and divide it in half crosswise at the perforation. Unroll each half and place the halves end-to-end on a lightly floured surface. Pinch the dough firmly to seal all of the seams. Lightly sprinkle flour on top of the dough and roll it out slightly. Transfer the dough to the baking pan, curving the dough in a lizard shape to fit in the pan.

STEP # **3** Pour the pizza sauce over the dough to within 1" of the edges. Decide where you want the lizard's tail to begin. Arrange the sausage and mozzarella and Parmesan cheeses to within 1" of the edges over just the head and body areas. Add a small amount of cheese to the tail area. Carefully fold the 2 long sides of the head and body so they meet in the middle; pinch firmly to seal the seams. Overlap the tail section, making it narrower than the body. Round off the head; squeeze the area between the head and body to make it smaller.

STEP # **4** Use the second roll of dough to patch any areas that may have torn and to create legs. Roll 4 pieces of dough to shape the legs, pressing down on one end to shape the feet. Use scissors to cut the feet to create toes. Position the legs on the lizard.

STEP # **5** Beat the egg yolk and brush it evenly over the entire lizard. Add the olive slices for the eyes. Place the red peppercorns in the center of the olive slices. Attach the black peppercorns for the nostrils. Cut the roasted red pepper into a forked tongue and add it to the lizard.

STEP # **6** Bake for 15-20 minutes or until golden brown.

added grossness!

Create "road kill" lizard by pushing down or smashing part of the lizard so the pizza sauce oozes out.

Royal Flush

Makes 1 freshly cleaned commode

You're no potty 'til some potty loves you.

You'll Need

1 (3 oz.) pkg. blue gelatin
1 purchased or prepared
    7" round angel food cake
2 (16 oz.) tubs white frosting

2 purchased or prepared
    7" angel food cake loaves
Black food coloring

Directions

STEP # 1 Prepare gelatin according to package directions. Refrigerate until nearly firm.

STEP # 2 Carefully enlarge the hole in the angel food cake, leaving a 2" border of cake around the outside to create a toilet bowl. Reserve the cut-away pieces of cake. Frost the inside of the cake.

STEP # 3 Carefully cut away a small vertical slice from the back side of the round cake to make a flat back. Reserve the cut-away piece. Frost the flat back side of the cake.

STEP # 4 Frost 1 long side of each angel food cake loaf. Set 1 loaf on the serving tray with the frosted side against the flat back of the round cake. Frost the top of that loaf. Stack the other loaf in the same way. Frost the entire cake, setting aside ¼ cup of frosting. Using a knife, score a line all the way around the top loaf cake about 1" from the top to create the appearance of the tank lid. Score a line all the way around the round cake about 1" from the top to create the appearance of a toilet seat.

STEP # 5 Cut a piece of the reserved cake to fit in the bottom of the toilet bowl. From another of the reserved cake pieces, cut a small handle shape. Add a tiny amount of black food coloring to the reserved ¼ cup of frosting to tint it gray. Frost the handle and attach it to the toilet tank with extra frosting.

STEP # 6 Stir the gelatin vigorously and carefully spoon into the hole of the cake to create blue toilet water.

4 added grossness!

Replace blue gelatin with yellow gelatin and float mini chocolate candy bars in the gelatin. Serve with a roll of toilet paper instead of napkins.

Take a deep breath –
you're done.

Fly Strips

Makes 3 sticky, icky strips of fly paper

Bzzz... SPLAT! Who wants a snack?

You'll Need

3 yellow Fruit by the Foot
candies* or 9 yellow Laffy
Taffy candies, unwrapped ————> the Fly Strips

Various candies and nuts** ————> the Bugs

Directions

STEP #**1** If you're using Fruit by the Foot, simply unroll the candy to the length you want the fly strip.

STEP #**2** If you're using Laffy Taffy, stack 3 candies on top of each other and microwave for a few seconds at a time until they're soft and pliable. Keeping them stacked, pull and stretch to the length you want the fly strip. Using a pizza cutter or a sharp knife, trim off the ends and sides to even them out.

STEP #**3** Now start creating the flies and other flying insects. Using Chuckles or other sticky candy works well since the fly strip and the Chuckles stick together easily. To get nuts to stick, simply put a tiny piece of a Chuckles candy on the back side and adhere. You can get as creative as you'd like by crushing a light-colored, semi-transparent Life Savers candy and using any "wing-shaped" pieces to adhere to the bugs for wings.

STEP #**4** Start splattering the bugs on the fly strip, adding as many as you'd like. The more you add, the grosser it gets.

You can get some really interesting bugs/flies by pulling off small pieces of black Chuckles candies using a toothpick. By stretching the pieces slightly while applying them to the fruit by the foot, it gives the appearance of wings.

*We used Fruit by the Foot Flavor Kickers in Tropical Twist and removed the bottom orange section, leaving the yellow section exposed.
**We used black Chuckles candies, sunflower nuts and pineapple Life Savers.

There aren't any real flies on there, are there?
You'd better look closely!

Other Icky Recipes

Don't be scared of a little "ick."

Pus Pockets
Pick a pack of pus-filled pimples by filling hollowed-out and drained cherry tomatoes with softened flavored cream cheese. At serving time, "pop" the pimples by squeezing the tomatoes just enough so that the cream cheese "pus" oozes out. The joy is in the popping!

Tongues on Toast
Cut tongue shapes from a slice of bologna. Make a slight groove down the center using the back of a butter knife. Cut a closed-mouth shape from a slice of bread and cut a slit between the upper and lower lips. "Paint" the lips with butter, ketchup or mustard if you'd like. Place the narrow end of the bologna tongue through the slit in the bread and place the whole thing on a greased baking sheet. Bake at 350° about 10 minutes or until the bread and bologna are toasted. Licking your lips never tasted so good!

Dirty Worms
Follow the directions for Wiggling Worms on pgs. 42-43 except crush enough Oreo cookies to make 1-2 cups of crumbs (AKA dirt). Layer dirt and worms in a glass dish or small galvanized metal bucket. Serve immediately before they slither away!

Snake Bites

For each snake, cook 6-8 pieces of rigatoni pasta following the package directions. Rinse in cold water and drain. To make colored snakes, soak the cooked pasta for 5-10 minutes in enough cool water and food coloring to cover the pasta. Drain and dry. To make striped snakes, dip a toothpick in barbeque sauce and use it to draw snake markings along the top of each uncolored rigatoni piece. Fill each pasta piece with canned squeeze cheese. For each snake, place 6-8 cheese-filled pasta pieces end-to-end in a curvy snake shape. Cut the end of the last piece at an angle for the tail. Use barbeque sauce to "glue" on peppercorns for eyes. Using a vegetable peeler, remove one thin strip of carrot for each snake and cut a triangle from one end for a forked tongue. Place each in the mouth of a snake. Be sure to get your fingers out quick!

Eyeball Ice Cubes

Place 1 blueberry in each compartment of an ice cube or ice ball tray. Add water to the compartments and freeze until solid. Use these eyeball ice cubes to chill your favorite drink. Just don't turn your back on them!

Moldy Mac & Cheese

Make a batch of macaroni and cheese. Remove a small amount of the mac & cheese and place it in a small bowl. To the small bowl, add a little green and black food coloring to achieve a nice moldy color. Add a little food coloring to a small amount of dried bread crumbs. Fold the "moldy" mac & cheese lightly into areas of the plain mac & cheese and randomly sprinkle that area with the "moldy" bread crumbs. Mmmmold!

Index